THE DAILY ROUND

Other Books by Phillip Lopate

Poetry

The Eyes Don't Always Want to Stay Open (SUN)

Fiction

In Coyoacan (Swollen Magpie Press)

Non-Fiction

Being With Children (Doubleday)

THE DAILY ROUND

New Poems by
Phillip Lopate

New York 1976

Many of these poems appeared previously in *The Village Voice, Z, Sun, First Issue, Broadway Boogie, New, The Framingham Review, Telephone, Liberation, The Four Zoas, The New York Art Review,* and in the Phillip Lopate Issue, *Blue Pig 22.*

Design by Leonard Lopate

Photographs by Susan Opotow

ISBN 0-915342-14-6 (paperback)
ISBN 0-915342-15-4 (hardcover)

Library of Congress Catalog Card No. 76-7709

First Edition

The publication of this book is supported by a grant from the National Endowment for the Arts in Washington, D.C., a Federal agency.

To Pasternak

Contents

Part I — Not Sadness, Which Is Always There

Indigestible   5
Numbness   7
The Dowagers of New York   9
Film Noir   11
The Bum   13
Canto LXXXIX   14
It's Painful Getting Letters   16
Indian Winter   17
Not Sadness Which Is Always There   18
Yellow Bird   19
Allende   21

Part II — Childhood, Boyhood, Youth

Blue Pants   25
Rumours   33
Charlotte Russe   35
Once Long Ago   38

Part III — The Singles

The People on the First Floor   43
Furnished Room   44
Saturday on the West Side of Assisi   46
It's Good We Only See Each Other Once a Week   47
The Thrill of the First Night   48
Ode to Senility   49
The Woman Who Cried for Nothing   51
The Beautiful and the Ugly (A Play)   52
Penelope in Soho   54
Sulky Sonnet   55
The Time We Stayed in the Dead Artist's Shack   56
The Court of the Two Sisters   57
The Deer Flies   58

Someone in London   60
Hearts   62

Part IV — Meditations

September Sundown   65
In the Dentist's Chair   67
The Last Slow Days of Summer   75
The Truth That Hurts   78
The Daily Round   83

PART I

NOT SADNESS, WHICH IS ALWAYS THERE

Indigestible

A friend called up saying he was in a pre-suicidal mood.
I told him to come over.
I'd pay for the taxi.
"Will you go back with me to my apartment if I start to panic?"
I told him I would.
He arrived feeling chipper.
He wanted some wine.
I gave him a little cold sauterne that had been sitting
    around in the icebox three weeks.
He said it tasted sour.

He looked at all my photographs.
He said he was feeling better.
We went out to dinner,
But it had to be on Madison Avenue.
For some reason he trusted Madison Avenue whereas
    Lexington, Third, Second and York were out to get him.
We sat in the last table far away from any draught.
I had my eyes on the delicatessen floor.
The radio was full of George Wallace being shot.
"Just like Huey Long," said my friend.
"Nixon did it
Now the gangsters are in the White House!"
I didn't argue.
My eyes were on my plate, Stuffed Derma and french fries.
Indigestible.
Suddenly he asked: "Are you feeling closer to me...?"

Of course I was,
I loved him.
But I used different words so as not to frighten him.
His head vibrated like a top whirling so fast you can't see it
    spin.
We paid the check and I told him as we were walking along
    Fifth Avenue, to catch the park and its rusty sunset, that
    I was also going through a bad time.

I had pinned my hopes on a shallow woman.
Though I no longer wanted her I felt curiously enervated.
Why this pain in my abdomen.
"Very simple," explained my friend.
"You experience an expansion, joy, the energy flows into all
    parts of the body.
Then a contraction, blocked, everything goes to the stomach.
You're still in high energy.
But there's no release.
The result is despair."
"That's it exactly!" I said to him.
It was getting darker and the first fat raindrops spattered
    onto the canopies.
The doormen were slipping inside, I was too excited to care.
"Answer me one more thing: expansion, contraction,
    physiology, I understand perfectly.
But what is it that stops us, when we're so near to joy?"

Only now did I notice my friend had his mad look.
His eyes, always beautiful, slid into passing cars.
He begged me to stop talking but I wouldn't.
I challenged him to explain the connections.
This nightfall, the orange chocolate smell, the dumpy couple
    walking by.
"Look at them," he said. "They're not going crazy.
Because they're healthy?
Or because they can't feel enough, because they don't know
    how to feel it."

Just then I felt it!
Right through my body.
"I feel it! I know what you mean! I feel it too!"
I wanted him to know...
"I don't think I'll wait for a bus," he said and jumped into a
    cab.
His face wobbled against the wet glass.

The next day he was still alive.
Still alive.

Numbness

I have not felt a thing for weeks
But getting up and going to work on time
I did what needed to be done, then rushed home.
And even the main streets, those ancient charmers,
Failed to amuse me, and the fight between
The upstairs couple was nothing but loud noise.
None of it touched me, except as an irritation,
And though I knew I could stop
And enjoy if I wanted to
The karate excitement and the crowd
That often gathers in front of funeral homes,
I denied myself these dependable pleasures,
The tricks of anti-depression
That had taken me so long to learn,
By now worn smooth with use, like bowling alleys in my soul.
And certain records that one can't hear without
Breaking into a smile, I refused to listen to
In order to find out what it would be like
To be cleansed of enthusiasm,
And to learn to honor my emptiness,
My indifference, myself at zero degrees.

More than any desire to indulge the numbness
I wanted to be free of the bullying urge to feel,
Or to care, or to sympathize.
I have always dreaded admitting I was unfeeling
From the time my father called me 'a cold fish,'
And I thought he might be right, at nine years old
And ever since I have run around convincing everyone
What a passionate, sympathetic person I am.

I would have said no poetry can come
From a lack of enthusiasm; yet how much of my life,
Of anyone's life, is spent in neutral gear?
The economics of emotions demand it.

Those rare intensities of love and anguish
Are cheapened when you swamp them with souped-up
                                    ebulliences,
A professional liveliness that wears so thin.
There must be a poetry for that other state
When I am feeling precisely nothing, there must
Be an interesting way to write about it.
There are continents of numbness to discover
If I could have the patience or the courage.

But supposing numbness were only a disguised
                                    disappointment?
A veil for anger? Then it would have no right to attention
In and of itself, and one would always have to push on,
Push on, to the real source of the trouble—
Which means, back to melodrama.
Is the neutral state a cover for unhappiness,
Or do I make myself impatient and unhappy
To avoid my basic nature, which is passive and low-key?
And if I knew the answer,
Would it make any difference in my life?
At bottom I feel something stubborn as ice fields,
Like sorrow or endurance, propelling me.

The Dowagers of New York

1.

The dowagers of New York in Persian lamb
with orange scarves around stringmeat necks
turn up at every movie matinee,
then fall asleep in their seats.
"I wasted three dollars on this tripe."

At the ballet, the opera,
"I doze. It's nothing.
I like to listen with my eyes closed."

2.

New York is an Eastern European city,
a kingdom for dowagers' faces.
Old lady, you have the profile
of a mighty statesman, Disraeli.
But what happened to the rest of your body?
The middle went away.
And now you look so clutchy in the crosstown bus,
trying to win approval from the old woman next to you
with swollen legs who nods, shakes her head,
without really listening to a word.

  "I have an extra ticket to the Noel Coward play;
it's supposed to be very well done.
This is where I get off. March 28th on a Saturday,
can you come? Don't forget!
Mark it in your calendar book!"
                                        She's on the sidewalk

Now where? Some coffee,
a little lunch, a napoleon.
She takes her sweet tooth very seriously.

So wealthy and so foolish, how does she manage
to get through the weeks, waiting while
her husband rounds out his last years of practice?

   Her wiser sisters have all flown South,
leaving her, like a retarded starling
in this cold museum city, the Moscow of America
to peck at a few crumbs
of pastry and culture.

Film Noir

For Tom Luddy

A large-shouldered man with short hair fingers his hat
While a beautiful woman paces impatiently in her
    morning-robe
With a cigarette burning beneath lipstick mouth.
— "What's this about your husband, Miss?"
— "That isn't why I called you here." She fixes him a drink.
The man lets his creased hat drop on the coffee table.
He can take in the house at a glance.
There are lamps on end-tables, mail-order furniture,
Glass animals and liquor, but no books,
And everything has been pushed into corners.
The place is too dark. Venetian blinds speckled with soot.
And the curtains are never quite open.
A two-step from the living-room is the bedroom.

Ah, lonely American decor of working-class houses near
    train tracks,
Where the men go off for days on railroad runs
And the wives pace in lowcut negligees, smoking
And plotting murder.

She wasn't evil, she wasn't a killer, she was just
Born poor and didn't know any better
So she grabbed the first man she could
After her boss got tired of her.
She grabbed a big hunk of man, ugly but honest;
He made an honest living, drove a big brute locomotive
But how could she have known that big-shouldered
Didn't mean good in bed. In fact he was a disaster.
Then the man in the hat came along.
He also had big shoulders, but he was good in bed.

They thought of running away together
But without money they wouldn't get far.
And poverty was no lark, she knew that; soon they'd
Turn on each other and life would be wretched.
So she figured out a plan. At first he didn't want to
Go along with it, because her husband was an all-right guy
But soon she persuaded him with her passionate figure
Which she paraded before him day and night in corset stays,
And her lipstick mouth sapped him, he knew lust;
And he got tired of meeting in hotel rooms to make love,
And besides, he was a weak character, though he could
Lift a sink, but from a moral point of view, he was weak.

Well, that's the story. They both got the electric chair.
In one version she gets accidentally strangled by a telephone
    cord.
In another he disappears and hits Skid Row unshaven.
But always there's that haunting smoke, between railroad cars
Where they go to ditch the body,
And always there's that flesh-love, that no one can take away.

The Bum

Recently I saw a raggedy bum
take out his dick in the subway
and prepare to piss against the tile wall

Then he saw me and shrugged
as if to say, What can I do, I'm a failure
I can't hold it in

I should figure out a way to write this as a haiku

Canto LXXXIX

"How much are you paying for your place?"

"Too much. 180."

"That's not bad for a studio. I've seen worse."

"I've seen worse also. I've looked at studios for 230."

"It's crazy."

"Sure it's crazy. For one little room and a kitchenette? You could rent a whole house for that."

"You're paying for the convenience of living in midtown."

"I think I'd rather live in the country."

"You said you didn't want to be in the country."

"I'm not so sure about this setup anymore."

"You think you'll try the country eventually?"

"Who knows?"

"A friend of mine got a one-bedroom apartment with a backyard and fixed it up beautiful."

"How much was she paying?"

"I think it was $325."

"Well, sure."

"It really looked beautiful. That's the only way you can get a nice place."

"On my salary the rent I'm paying now is already too much for me."

"I thought teachers made good money."

"I make just enough. If he raises the rent on me I'll be in trouble."

"How much can he raise it by?"

"Seven per cent?"

"I think the maximum is fifteen per cent."

"Fifteen per cent is a lot. On 180 that's what—$30?"

"No. Ten per cent is $18. Fifteen per cent would be 18 plus 9. $27. Still, that's a lot to pay for your studio: two hundred and seven dollars."

"I'll have to move out."

"Lofts are expensive too. Just in the last few years the

prices of lofts have skyrocketed. Everybody's looking for a loft."

"Everybody's looking, period."

"It's true, that's the problem. Everybody's looking. And then they want key money."

"I won't give any key money."

"Sometimes you have to. A friend of mine got a fantastic four-room place for $86 a month. But she had to slip the janitor $1500."

"It's unfair, $86 a month."

"I don't even like to go over and visit. I sit on the couch eating my heart out."

"That's what gets me so furious. You pay lavish rents and you get nothing in return. Nothing. Nothing! I would sooner buy into a town house with other people."

"That's not a bad idea, a town house."

"I don't know if a town house is such a great idea either."

"And town houses can be very expensive too."

It's Painful Getting Letters

It's painful getting letters from those
you love only a little, and who
think you're their best friend.
They write you four page laments and you
return one, three months later
full of hasty regrets.
You would like to love them completely
for what they are, as their mother loved them
(or didn't love them), but as you watch them flounder
in blandness and self-pity from one world capital to the next,
you can't escape the thought that they can do nothing for
    you,
unless it be to teach you a little more about
the sinking strategies of survival.
Each letter ends with a more passionately imagined
    rendezvous
which begins to sound like a threat:
"Have so much to tell in person—
I hope to come up through New Hampshire this July."
"Maybe we'll visit Denmark after all!"
So by now you can see inside out the day when
you two *will* be together, facing the stream
and pretending that beautiful Nature has made you silent.

Indian Winter

Inferior to the day,
Which is beautiful and mild,
Unseasonably gentle,
I cross the park
Observing nothing,
Alone in my mind,
On a Saturday afternoon,
With everyone strolling
To catch the sun
And almost against
My will I notice
A young man with a baby
Riding on his back,
Two old ladies in my way,
And I am thinking:
"Come on, you must.
Of course live."
That was no noble decision,
No more than a marble
Dropped onto the sidewalk
Continues to roll.

Not Sadness Which Is Always There

After I had learned to live with my sadness
There came another, more disturbing strangeness
Whose purpose I could never understand, who always came
                                                    late at night

And who kept me awake all hours
Until I turned on the headlamp to read,
As if finally forced to give in,

Not understanding that some things have nothing to do with
                                                    the Will.
I who had conducted my life so that
I could not do other than what I do,

Who had steered my heavy ship around and around
Until it could only steer in one direction,
I saw no way to put this turmoil to good use.

It was not sadness, which is always there
like a cat I raised from childhood and stroke absent-mindedly
While going on with my work;

Not even loneliness, which I had trained to back down
In the presence of good company,
But something more needy.

Even as I sit with friends in the Hungarian pastry shop
Dawdling over sweets,
I am shaken by the urge to run home

To be alone with it, to let it work me over,
The mice combing the bag of day-old crumbs
Raking my stomach for overlooked mistakes.

Yellow Bird

The day after Thanksgiving I went into the Drago Shoe Shine Parlor to get my once a year shine. The streets were churning with bloated strollers on holiday, their bodies dulled by half-digested turkey, and faces with thoughtful frowns attentive to the lower regions. Slowed down overnight, they had evolved into a race of philosophers. The owner of the shoe store stood in the doorway looking for something bright to catch his eye.

I took possession of my throne without much fuss. The red stuffed vinyl gave out a hiss when I sat down. I would have loved to prolong this imperial moment by reaching to my left for a magazine, but unfortunately I was the only customer. A black in a short-sleeved green uniform began to apply himself to my feet, without any personal bitterness, but philosophically, sudsing the corners with a peachy mush.

Leaning against the display counter was a young Jamaican I had not noticed before. He was brownskinned, and dressed in a very sporty outfit—jockey cap, lemon jacket, tight-fitting lemon pants. It was not so much that the costume was dramatic as that it seemed so coordinated, so up-to-date, so cunning and yet unimpeachably correct. Almost, I found myself thinking, like a pimp's outfit.

Suddenly he began to sing.

> Yellow bird, why do you fly away?
> Yellow bird, why do you fly away?
> Did your little wife
> Leave your little nest?
> Did she fly away
> Leaving you to stay?...

He sang the song right through, crooning it with impeccable suaveness like Nat King Cole, and the breezes that blow through an island beach. No one gave the slightest indication of hearing him, least of all the burly man brushing my shoes. The singer's own eyes were sullen, opaque, refusing to give in to the lyrics of the song. The song flew out of him against his will; its moment had come to escape. If he were being handcuffed at that moment he would sing it, if he were being led away, if he were standing beside the grave of his mother he would have to sing the silly song about the yellow bird.

Da da da da da...what does he care about the yellow bird? What did the bird ever do for him? It is possible that he beats women across the face, it is quite possible that they would give anything to see him once in this tender mood which breaks out only in the rarest moments of self-forgetfulness, leaning against a shoe counter, waiting for a business appointment.

And when he finished the last note, he walked straight out of the store.

Allende

In 200 years they won't remember me, Salvador
And they won't remember you, so let's skip the part about
He will live with us forever.
You may get a footnote for being the only Marxist
To gain power in Latin America via parliamentary means;
And the only sucker not to throw his enemies in jail.
You knew the power of the large land-owners, ITT,
The Army, U.S. Anaconda, the small frightened
      businessmen
Easily manipulated, the shop-owners who could go either
      way
And yet you didn't lift a finger to silence them.
You continued to defend the bicameral system of government
Until they bombed your palace and you shot yourself in the
      mouth.
Answer me this,
Now that you are a bunch of hairs on a blood-stained sofa:
I want to know why you killed yourself.
Because this was a very un-Marxist thing to do.
Because neither was this the way of a gradualist
With short graying hair and glasses,
      and a face like a prominent surgeon's,
Who, knowing this would happen, could have easily
      arranged for
The secret tunnel, the private plane, the unmarked car
In which you, huddled in grandmotherly wig, might begin
To write your memoirs. Was it too horrible to think of
Speaking at New York rallies to pockets of émigrés,
Forming shadow cabinets, and lunching with Juan Bosch
Or Andreas Papandreou, swapping stories over wine about
Where you were when the shit hit the fan?
I'm being vulgar, forgive me.
I would rather believe in your doggish retreat
Than the flamboyance of today's headlines which gloat:
MARXIST REPORTED TO TAKE HIS LIFE.
Even they are a little unsure. They leave room

for the graduate students
Of the left, working in the carrels of libraries
For 100 years to discover the link,
The way it all fits together: Lumumba, King, Kennedy,
    Allende, CIA.

And it may turn out that my government actually murdered
    you
But what's the good of knowing that?
We know too many connections already, and they only satisfy
The pedantic urge that makes the world a crossword puzzle.
Salvador, I'm sorry, I don't know what to say any more.
Take back the bullet, it was a mistake, it redeems nothing.

Today I look at the faces of passers-by and I think:
It figures. The banks have the money to buy counter-
    revolution,
This wino has no money. He's nice enough, so is
That girl in the flamingo summer dress on wobbly heels.
It's September 12, possibly the prettiest day of the year.
The blue has never been so pure around the chimneys—
"Almost like—a cartoon!" says the dental hygienist,
Grasping for a metaphor. I never said it even to myself,
Before today, but just between you and me,
And I don't want anyone else to hear:
    Señor,
It looks as if they have got us by the balls.
These faces in the street, how can they take power?
How can they rule?

PART II

CHILDHOOD, BOYHOOD, YOUTH

Blue Pants

If you follow your feet
                    you end up in the marketplace
                    because that's all you want
                       is the crush of slobs
                      drooling black sausage
                              grease
            on table after oilcloth covered table

Orchard Street Petticoat Lane the Plaka la Marqueta
                    les Marchés aux Puces
               with the gypsy scarves   old suits
               78 gramophone records
      Empty Saturday processions through church bazaars
               looking for a silver saltshaker
               or a shoelace
                       but it had to be the right shoelace

In Amsterdam once the sorethroat Dutch rain
                    caught up with me in an open market
                    soaked the shishkebabs
                              sizzled the fires
                    tarps tented down over stands

A badtempered afternoon   with nothing to say for it
          I had time to kill
                       before night
      when the women took up their doorways under red light
               bulbs along the canal
                    The water is black
               and it came as a shock
                         to find my pocket picked
          though later on it all made sense

               What did I expect?

Anyway, marketplaces:
I started going when I was a boy
My mother took me to the city market
        where Havemeyer Street ended, in Brooklyn

Ladies lowering their shopping carts
                inch by inch
                        over the curb
                careful with the eggs on top

Some little coughing girl was always getting it
        "COVER YOUR MOUTH!"   I felt glad
                                it wasn't me

    Childhood is standing by the curb
waiting for a lady to finish
talking to another lady
in a flower print dress
wondering if it's safe
to cross the street
    Sometimes you get a smack

    But I hold on because   it's worse
                        to lose my mother's hand
            and run up and down
                    vegetable stalls
    with a few tears and the briny smell of
            sour pickles making me hungry
And "Damn! Damn! where'd my mother go?"
                        cursing bad luck
        while trying to look grownup and curious
                        for the others

It all comes back later in a funny dream
    the one where I'm walking along the thoroughfare
        with my heart's delight   and the camera moves
            a little to the right
                    a closeup of my smile

so that I don't even notice love
　　passing out of the frame
　　like the railing of a streetcar
until I realize her hand is gone
and there's nothing else to notice
　　　　　　or to mourn

But I wanted to tell you the story about the blue pants.
I'm determined to get that story out of the way
　　　　Do you suppose a new life
　　　　　　　　　could start for a man
　　　　　　　　　if he told an anecdote perfectly?
A story, let's say
　　　　that clouds his thoughts for years
　　　　　　　　　until one day he shouts
　　　　Enough! Get away from me!
　　　　I don't care any more about the blue pants!
　　　　　　You could strangle me   I'm not
　　　　　　　　telling it again
　　　　I'll write it down once, then leave me alone.

My mother had taken me to the marketplace
　　to buy a new pair of pants.
Try to imagine what embarrassment for an eight year old boy
　　to have his mother apprise his figure
　　　　　　　　　an entire afternoon
Nothing could be worse, you'd think.
I was looking forward to it.
　　　　　　The gypsy ladies in windbreakers
　　　　　　　　　　tried to catch her eye
　　　　　　　　with velvet swatches   calico
　　　　　　　　　　　　　housedresses
　　　　　"Something for the young man?
　　　　　　　　Earmuffs?"
　　　but this time she skipped all the street bargains
　　　　　　and took me into a decent store.

The man had a measuring tape
around his shoulders
Bushy mustache bushy eyebrows
sunken eye sockets
and only half an inch taller than me.
How could it be otherwise with the shop
so narrow that only a runt could pass between
the suitracks and the shelves
jutting with boxes
half shoved-in shoved-out

"What color is he looking for?"
"Something in black or charcoal grey," I heard
my mother say.
"Step this way."

Then I saw a pair of blue cotton pants
the most beautiful pants in my life
A royal blue
that sopped up all the joy in the ocean
and mocked the sooty dark Brooklyn clouds

How could you be sad
knowing you had a pair of such wild pants
to put on next morning
and make the rounds with?

like the blue porthole that hypnotizes you
like the blue shark,
that kind of blue

"Don't you think?" said
my mother, "they're a little too loud?"
I knew right away
that whatever she was trying to tell me
was no good for the blue pants.

But what was her objection?
The salesman and she seemed to share the joke
"Take it from me cookie you don't want these pants.
They look awfully good to you now
                                                but in a week
you'll be tired of them. They're—*garish*,
                                        you understand?"
                    Garish? Loud?
        I understood that she had the money.
                        Without a struggle   too proud
                    I let them slip from my hands.
        Let me turn my face from their blinding blue ray
let me examine these charcoal greys
these browns my mother said
go good with my eyes.
Maybe even this old man pinstripe
                    has something to say for it.

    Sad business herringbone   O lugubrious worsteds
        though I took several from the pile of
                        distinguished weaves,
                they were heavy and I wanted to
            float light and cottony above the world!

    In the cardboard dressing room
                with three brass hooks
    I let my khaki chinos shiver to the floor
                Poor chinos I had also loved you once
                        thought you'd open every door for me
    Now you were used up and I
            sweating in baggy wool
            before two mirrors that caught my profile
    at an angle I never wanted to see again
                the crooked nose, the cowlick
        the earnest earnest Austrian cadet's eyes—
                                    listening to my mother
            behind the partition flirt with the salesman
    talking about children's wear and the high cost of meat

I surprised her.
"Those aren't bad. Turn around...
They're a little baggy around the seat."
I went back
and tried on the brown with droopy pleats.
I was curious how much ugliness
she would make me swallow.

> "I like that color on you" she said
> "How do they fit?"
> They fit okay, I shrugged.
> (I wasn't giving much.)

She whispered me into a nest of suits.
> "Listen, I know you still feel bad
> about the blue pants. Right?"
> > "No I forgot about them."
> "The reason I wouldn't let you have them
> > is that those are the pants,"
> > > she lowered her voice,
> > "all the Puerto Ricans wear.
> They're gaudy! not in good taste
> > You don't want to go around
> > looking like a Puerto Rican do you?"

"No." I looked at her level and innocent
till shame had filled her chubby face,
like cherry Kool Aid in a pitcher.
She was not a bigoted woman, she tried to be enlightened,
she did the best she could in raising us.
I stick to this banner
though all the schools of psychotherapy leer
though Panzer tanks of women shrinks
roll over her fallen shield in their efforts
to embrace me, I stick to this
to my last dying breath: For all her faults
My mother was essentially *not a bad woman*.

I wanted that shameful look in her eyes to go away
I wished I could find a new pair of pants
and fall in love with them, earnestly
so that my mother would feel all right.
But I couldn't.
My face was sulking.
There was nothing I could do about my face!

"Look,
you still want those crazy blue ones?
Try them on."

I snatched them into the dressing room
before she could change her mind.
Now comes the part I don't know how to tell.
Maybe I had waited too long.
Like a beautiful underwater rock
the diver brings up to the surface
only to watch its vibrant colors fade
in the air, that brilliant blue
died a little when I put it on.
I suddenly understood
how common they were.

Love
            had played its first trick on me
I was frightened by my own fickleness
How could I know that the radiance comes and goes?
I didn't have the heart to admit
that I no longer cared for them
There was no turning back now
                  I put on a brave smile of gratitude
and issued forth   ready
                  to convince her that she had made me
the happiest boy

My mother was in terrific spirits
She came home and told everyone
            how she had indulged my cockeyed tastes
The neighbors said,
            he has to learn
                        by his own mistakes
            They had a good laugh

I stored the pants on a hanger
way back in the closet
where I could barely reach them
Once or twice I wore my blue pants to school
I wished them an evil fate

and was glad
when I found them
kicked and tarstained on the closet floor

            So much for getting what you want, I thought
            and closed the door on happiness
                  for many years

            Maybe that's an exaggeration
            Anyway you've heard the story
                  Some story, eh?

            Probably I didn't tell it right
I still don't know whether to feel charmed or angry!

        Scars end up as decorations
                it doesn't matter—
                In this life, who knows
                who will have the final word,
                the hurt or the blue?

Rumours

The whole fifth grade was
suddenly amok with love
Someone had thrown Jonas
against Teresa
in a game of catch-the-girls
And Jonas said I'm sorry
She'd felt her arm slide over his
Next Saturday he took her
to the movies—or so she says
and bought her a bracelet
with two hearts, and
a stuffed felt lion.

Meanwhile David had thrown over
serious-minded Tanya
and showed interest in Wanda,
his former enemy—
after telling everyone
he couldn't stand her guts.
And Wanda knew David's telephone number
by heart.
She told it to her cousin
who called David and said:
What do you think of Wanda?
And David screamed:
I can't stand her guts!
But Wanda knew he'd asked her out
and had to keep their secret
from the world,
and that was just his way.

The others who were not involved
in this romantic life—
the slow ones, the workers,
the short boys—

hated the lovers and called them
brown-noses.
They thought that love meant
sticking one's nose
up a girl's behind.
But Christine, the tall mild grownup
girl who wrote about horses,
thought everyone was acting very childish,
and wondered if the teacher
needed help straightening off
her desk, which looked a mess,
or marking present-and-absent
in the rollbook.

Charlotte Russe

Charlotte Russe, whipped cream with a dab of shortcake
    inside a cardboard hatbox
                which
      turned over
            reveals a false bottom
   Half cake half air
      dissolving in the mouth on contact
no matter how you try to prolong it

         A cheat   this Charlotte
      like Marlene in *The Scarlet*
Empress whose crinolines and
               rouge
      beguile horsemen down staircases
        to the
           grotto bedroom
    where they clutch
          a phantom flesh
all gauze and veils   a trick
    like the obliging women who open
  their dresses to you in dreams

Old whipped cream swindle
     But what's more fun
   than to be taken with your eyes open

It was in my senior year
    I had passed my Algebra regents.
       I left the muddy doors
   of the high school entrance
crowded with grubs comparing answers—as if
        that could help them now

and thinking I deserved a special gift
for getting such a high mark
on a test which, after all,
            "wasn't even my subject"
I bought myself for fifteen cents
            a Charlotte Russe

That year I piled triumph upon triumph.
Exam after exam fell
before my magnetized pencil.
Valedictorian
Most Likely to Succeed
The Chamber of Commerce Award -
who could I take along my lonely walks
to share the raptures of
enumeration?
Self-astonished at every moment
I had no one to tell but
the elevated trains, roaring over me
like Gods with stomach pains

Where was my *equal*,
        where was there someone to join in my rejoicing,
    what was I supposed to do with this miraculous
                            energy?
I was so powerful I could shake the girders if I dared!

In the end it was painful.
You have to return to a
normal life.
I bought a Charlotte Russe
at the bakery under the El:

            A rush of sweetness
            then dissolution,
    disenchantment, the slow ironic smile relaxing
        to a more comatose well-being

Came graduation—
What speeches I gave!
when it ended I was more alone than ever
People clap to feel their palms smack together
Friends smiled but I kept looking for
the black dot in their eyeballs.
The parents you could forget about—
They knew too well how to spike
any compliment with their own lament

Only you, Charlotte
                        understood me
        You realized I wanted nothing more
                    than a little sweetness
                a kiss of gentle confection
            to ease me down to human scale,
                where I could disappear
                                    among the rest

            Not constancy   no special favors
        only that when I came to you   tired
            you would be fresh and worldly-wise

    and let me bury my nose in your white ermine muff!

Once A Long Time Ago

Once a long time ago, you remember
we were living in the basement of our parent's house
we two brothers, the girls sharing a room upstairs
It was dark in the basement, dark and hard to move around
and our sister charged her friends a dime
to visit, calling it the Spook House.
    I would look up from my book
sometimes and see a line of ten year olds
in pink shorts
climbing down the trap door steps.
What are you doing here? I asked calmly
never realizing I was the spookiest part of all
The little girls giggled and ran for help
Maybe you don't remember that
You were too busy looking for a job

    Maybe you remember how we slept together
next to the oil burner
on an old double mattress, getting along,
two friends, never complaining about privacy
until one afternoon around four-thirty
I came across you, my older brother, older
and ashamed to be living under his mother's roof,
your legs hanging out of a green, sour-smelling topsheet,
your black hair mussed, your stallion's eyes desperate
like horses trapped in a flaming barn.
You wouldn't look at me.
                        I asked you what was wrong
you remember? But instead of answering your whole body
    shrunk
and when I got into bed beside you
you started to cry   you started to cry but no sound came out
and I was wondering if you were faking
or if there was so much that wanted to come out
that you had to hold a pillow over it
    and smother it

I never told you this but Esquire Magazine was lying
on the floor face up, the new issue, and I wondered
if something you had seen there had made you unhappy
like the disgusting Bourbon ads, or the dense novelettes
that left me slightly nauseous like cups of warm water

I also wished I could look at the new issue
I had time for many thoughts because you took a while
    crying
and I couldn't think of anything to do except hold you
and keep asking what was wrong
I felt confident in the end you would tell me
and this is perhaps what you could never forgive me
My conqueror's belief in the absolute power of sympathy
because you never did tell me
and I saw that you didn't trust me enough
and I still don't know to this day
what was wrong
because all you said was
"Leave me alone, just leave me alone for two minutes."

PART III

THE SINGLES

The People on the First Floor

There must be a house where sunlight
falls on and on on the bedspread;
maybe a cherry tree outside,
and in the window ledge a kleenex box
with one lilac tissue collecting dust.
I keep looking into people's apartments on the first floor.
Red-flowered geraniums are common
and upholstered chairs with gold fringes and
families walking around in their undershirts.

It breaks my heart, those comfortable first floor interiors.
How they set up a reading corner with one cool blue lamp
against the heckling street,
the plump foot hassock resting there. . . .
But even mildewed Slavic tenements have their grace notes:
a calendar, a boy's toy car,
a meaty arm filling the windowsill.

Who are these citizens who consent to live
in full view, offering their placid ordinariness
to a city desperate for lucid models?
Maybe saints. Maybe cranks. Manikins?
They sit in the dark
and their furnishings overwhelm them
like the homey darkness that grows around a blind man.

Furnished Room

When you live in a furnished room
the world starts to resemble a furnished room.
Even when you go out on the street,
people with winter coats on look like furnished rooms.

Your room is never heated properly,
you are always chilly and hoping
to warm up in restaurants.
You buy a coffee, you make the pretense
of loving your paperback book,
an hour to waste before the show,
you grab at the immaculate bathroom
of a college student center
where you read a leaflet on the floor which means
absolutely nothing to you,
as if you were forced to repeat a course
in Spanish,
or take a long pleasure holiday in a rainy place.

Later you mingle near a crowd of strangers
at intermission.
Your skin is flushed and you listen to their conversation
and you are almost ecstatic and you
have to return to your furnished room
with the tall ceilings
which are unusual for their antique molding
but why does one need such a high ceiling?
Better to live under the bed than to have that high ceiling!

The night will find you, and the covered quilt
and the newscaster's voice
will seep in like an odorless gas,
and the upstairs boarder's shoes
will grind down on your chest,

and is it true that you are lost
in this one furnished room
with no home but this
And am I really lost, for good,
under the furnished stars

Saturday on the West Side of Assisi

Saturday morning put on a record make coffee
and dance in front of the mirror
You're not Fred Astaire but you'll do
as you whisper "I love I love I lo-ove her!"
but whom do you love, remember?
Saturday. Only Saturday.
The coffee smells good and you know exactly when to turn it
off.

Sip it on a stuffed chair looking at the thin light
spoon itself, like sugar, onto the dusty rose carpet
Those special pink dyes only the Chinese know —
This isn't one of them.
Can't get rugs like that out of Peking any more.

Later you water the plants and walk to the lake
Watch the long-distance runners with numbered orange
    tee shirts
and the slow lazy couples who have just got up from sex,
cruising the windows of antique shops for a lamp.
You come back home and read a long numbing article
in The New York Review of Books on Conrad
By that time it will be three o'clock and you've
run out of momentum. Time to make new decisions
get on the phone: Who wants to go to the movies tonight?

This is my life. I have no complaints.
If I were a family man I could spend weekends responding
to my children's cuts and yells,
never have to think too far in advance. Maybe lock myself
in the rec room for hours reading every word of Proust.
No, I'd be happy.
Grant that much to the future.
The birds
would hop above my deckchair in what suburban sunset?
But the birds sing even on West 71st Street,
and I am Saint Francis of Assisi.

It's Good We Only See Each Other Once a Week

It's good we only see each other once a week.
A young man about to move in with his fiancee
died of a sudden heart attack at twenty-six.
One hears these stories all the time.
The heart is trained to handle deprivation,
not unforeseen happiness. Just as when you
throw your arms around me I start to overflow,
but then I think of course, where was she before?
I deserve it and a lot more besides —
your love gets soaked up quickly
and I pull back brooding over something
I never had.
But don't stop on that account, keep going.

I was brought up to make
the most of accidental brushes with kindness.
My pleasures were collected almost unawares
from stationary models, like the girl
who sat in front of me in tenth grade,
who let me stroke and braid her golden hair
and never acknowledged it.
I wouldn't know what to do with frontal love;
would I? One snowy winter night in Montreal
I felt so great I danced a flamenco
and insisted that everyone call me Fernando.
But then I was by myself. And last night,
if there are many more nights
like last night with you —
when I think of all my nights of total happiness
I get the panicky sense that the balance
has already tipped,
and I will never again feel free
to pass myself off as a have-not.

Maybe it's good we only see each other once a week.
But don't stop on that account, keep going.

The Thrill of the First Night

I love the first night when I sleep with someone new
And even more I love the second night
But the third night can be problematical
The fourth night is enjoyable
In a quiet way
Though often it doesn't get to a fourth night

And after all the love has run its course
I love to walk around the girders
In a city park
Maybe holding up a viaduct or highway exit
And think that all this green, like so much cabbage
Or stinkweed on a humid day,
And the broken glass and fieldstone walls and steps
To walk down quickly looking over your shoulder,
Will still be around when they throw you over.

Ode to Senility

The ultraviolet night-light in the florist's
seen from a bedroom window, 6:15
Hour of furry dawn, no one is up yet
I leave the woman's house before her daughter wakes up
I wish I could tell this girl I mean her mother no harm
The woman goes back to sleep, I close the latch behind me
I am old, old, old
I start to fall asleep in the taxi
I climb the brownstone steps with a full bladder
With one gesture I fling off my coat and open the door
I am tired and I curl up on my bed
I am realizing my lifelong ambition, to grow old

I want to be eighty and have people whisper about me
in gatherings: He was a Communist,
he was the first to take acid
the earliest to recognize the System was rotten
And look how serenely he carries himself
such vibrant eyes   how well-preserved
these men of conviction remain!

Let them think I had a crazy youth
that blondes in furs beat down my door

I want to be eighty and tell anecdotes
the same five anecdotes
about the time I outwitted the tax service

I want to be old and tiresome and able
to forget those caresses
turning self-reflective on the thigh
forget the daughter in the next room

I know enough about the light behind the shadow behind the
    light

behind the marble on the terrace in the morning
and on everyone's faces

let me grow senile enough to watch
with gumless charity the pretty woman
squirming on a man's lap in the empty bus —
thinking,
Who are all these children who call me grandfather?
I don't remember marrying.
Which one of them did I finally love now,
Which one of them decided to put up with me?

The Woman Who Cried for Nothing

He introduced her to some friends in the street:
"This is a woman who cries for nothing."
Because after she flew to Sao Paolo to visit him
And the first day he was happy to see her;
And the second day he was pressed with life-worries;
And on the third day he was sad about
     taking a friend to the hospital
And the fourth day he threw his arms around her
     before everyone at the party and said,
       "How can we not live together?"
And the fifth day he never called;
And on the sixth he listened deeply like an African to music;
And the seventh he proposed
     that they go to a hotel and make love;
And on the eighth he would not help her buy a bus ticket;
And on the last day when she met him in the street,
He looked serene and vital and offered to carry her bags,
She burst into tears;
And he asked, "What are you crying for?"
And she said, "For nothing."

The Beautiful and the Ugly (A Play)

ACT 1.

Scene 1: A roomful of beautiful, stupid women making the most stupid conversation imaginable. One is telling fortunes from coffee grounds, another is complaining about a dirty spoon, and so on.

Scene 2: The couple in the restaurant. An ugly, brilliant man is talking to a ravishingly beautiful, stupid woman. The ugly, brilliant man is explaining about the Ottoman Empire.

Scene 3: A group of ugly, spiteful, brilliant women make sparkling conversation about the disappointments of love. They are a delight to listen to.

Scene 4: An ugly, brilliant woman and an ugly, brilliant man sitting in a restaurant. They analyze each other mercilessly.

ACT 2. The Half-Breed

Scene 1: A somewhat beautiful, somewhat homely, rather brilliant young woman is trying to fascinate an unbelievably good-looking rock 'n roll musician moron. In spite of the fact that the woman is wearing a scarlet satin blouse with the top four buttons unbuttoned, it is clear from certain gestures and dictions that she is a winner of a Woodrow Wilson Fellowship. The man asks her if she would like to smoke something, and she says "Sure."

Scene 2: The somewhat beautiful, somewhat homely, brilliant young woman is talking to her girl friend, another half-breed, and telling her the story of her date with the rock 'n roll moron. The friend listens silently with a knowing, judgmental half-smile. The story is that he has another girl-friend whom he lives with, but she managed to take him home with her. "He's extraordinarily sensitive in his own way. Uncanny—ability to know what I wanted. Not verbal—he's not very verbal, but an extraordinarily—odd use of language. I'm afraid I scared him." She giggles. Her friend keeps smiling.

Scene 3: A half-ugly, half-handsome, reasonably intelligent man flirts with a half-ugly, half-pretty, reasonably intelligent woman. They both confuse each other tremendously with double signals.

ACT 3.

Scene 1: A beautiful, brilliant, warm-hearted young woman appears. The playwright runs onto the stage and grabs her away, thus ending the play.

PERFORMANCE NOTE:

In the event it is impossible to find anyone suitable to play the part of the woman in Act 3, the play will be continued indefinitely, with the different characters combining and re-combining in any permutations that remain.

Penelope in Soho

You search his eyes for clues.
The loft bed that your husband built
So high it nailed you to the ceiling,
Before going off to spiritual India,
Now contains a second man.

'I want you to take me seriously.
Don't lie next to me and give me a taste of
The warm feelings I had learned to live without,
If you are only going to go away.'

You search his eyes for clues.
But everyone is going to go away.
At the end of the loft is a round brass gong
That the sunlight ripples like a goldfish
And he stares at it, stares for all he's worth.

Sulky Sonnet

The cypresses hang in the brackish fog
Outside our room. You don't get up all day,
Skin smelling acrid from cigarettes.
Wanna orange? Your bloodshot eyes take in
My simpleminded offer with distrust.
What's wrong? You can't explain, it goes too deep.
Your urge to live is down to thirty watts.
The window string flaps like a cripple's hand.
I'd love to ride a bike along the marina
All by myself, when sunset hits the water. . .
Then why do I stay cooped inside with you?
What holds me here? You don't want any chaperone
For this funk. You shut your eyes to doze
And I sit doting on your innocent toes.

The Time We Stayed in the Dead Artist's Shack

I wanted to lie in a casket beside you
And put my dead, reasonable flesh
Against your hysterical flesh, and row
Like two carved Vikings toward the stars

And I wanted you to love me for it.
You hid in the tub, in this house
With cows painted on bathroom walls
And Paradise murals in the empty room.

The Queen of Paradise was depicted as a naked eight year old
(The artist's daughter Mary had sat for it).
The shack was full of the dead man's work.
Murky easel paintings I could just barely see

In the dark of late afternoon thunderstorms.
I felt helpless, nauseous, puny
Waiting for you to get out of the tub,
Not sure at all I trusted you.

You washed your hair and sat for a moment
On my bed with a yellow towel around you,
And I reached out
Like a spider crawling toward the moonlight.

The Court of the Two Sisters

The slow green fans turning in the courtyard
Of the classy restaurant in New Orleans;
The green napkins and the Negro waiters
Advancing in their bright green uniforms, superiorly
Filling the large water goblets dusty in the sun.
The hot rolls with curled butter shells, like snails
And the enormous breakfasts served at all hours
Of Eggs with lemon sauce, asparagus, ham and toast points;
Cold creamed shrimp soup, oranges.
I read two newspapers at once, starting with sports;
Crowding the tablecloth with unwanted sections.
And when I was too stuffed to go on
I ordered a chickory coffee, dark and bitter
And a Charlotte Russe bursting with whipped cream.

The Deer Flies

They had taken me to a lone spooky spot,
An old beach where Indian pottery had been found,
Four thousand years old.
Sand crabs darted under dead timber.
The white sky glared whitely.
I stepped into the lukewarm Gulf Stream:
The tide was out, it was intolerably hot.
"You must find this oppressive," said Mary our hostess;
"The air is so close and still."

"Oh no," I said, "it's cool with my feet in the water."
Mary pointed out a rhinocerous beetle,
Then an armadillo hole. The flies were biting
At my legs and I had stupidly worn tennis shorts:
Baby blue shorts from Brooks Brothers!
Diane explained that the bugs were bad
When there was no wind. "It's a shame
There's no wind," said Mary. "It's usually
Not this buggy."

It started to rain. The rain bounced off
The calm ocean, slanty, and wattled the sand
like chicken pocks or alligator skin.
I ran for the car but they dawdled, remarking
How much they loved a good storm.
I could love a good storm too, I supposed,
Holding myself back, soaking on the hill
While the sky opened and they dug their toes
In the sand below, two Mississippi girls
Remembering exciting storms, pointing at the cloud:
"That white glare around the edges
Means rain won't cool it off one bit."

We made it to the car. There were flies
In the back seat, all over the styrofoam picnic basket.

"Those deer flies! They're terrible today," Mary swore.
But she wanted to show us a woods near the beach
That was even more unspoiled,
So we wandered down the dirt path through the trees,
Flies and dragontails at my face.
"Won't the rain make them go away?" I whined.
— "Where they going to go? When they're out, they're out."
The backs of my knees were swollen,
My arms itched like demons, and I was waving
Both hands in front of me just to get by,

"Who owns this land?" I demanded.
— "The property belongs to a real estate man
From New Orleans. His wife is a bit of a Bohemian
And she loves the country out here."
— "I hope she loves the bugs as well,"
I said testily. At that my hostess
Stopped and thought a bit:
"No. . . . I expect they stay in New Orleans
When the deer flies are out."

Someone in London

She had the whitest skin
and brown fingernail polish
and brown lipstick
and brownish red curly hair
and a dark brown satin skirt
and that marble-white skin
as if she were always about to faint
and she had a baby
and the baby had awfully white skin
and blonde hair
and the baby's father's name
was George
and he was somewhere in Brighton
trying to get back into school
And she was on Home relief
and she used to shoot heroin
and sometimes still did shoot heroin
when she ran into old bad friends
but then she felt guilty
for days, and nauseous.

She had once known a composer
of rock music when he was still
in art school, before he became big
whom she felt was the finest,
most sensitive, deeply shy person
and she told him, "I'm not
after anything, Brian. So don't
feel you have to sleep with me.
I just like coming around."
He didn't like women
though he had hundreds of them
so she stopped coming round.
Her mother bought her a pram

to push the baby in
She was studying the guitar
an hour a day
That's all.

Hearts

After we've played a noble scene
Where no one is blamed, and each
Takes the guilt for not loving enough,
You would think we would break up then and there.

We feel so fine and mature toward each other,
We could cry on the couch like the Idiot
In sympathy for everyone's point of view.

But after we've played our noble scene,
The empathy generates so much lust
That unfortunately, we patch it up
And two weeks later the real cut-throat stuff begins.

PART IV

MEDITATIONS

September Sundown

As long as the sun's up you are optimistic
A silence occupies the bedroom
Tomato plants in the garden — Indian summer

    The earnest boy with a face like an olive
rides his bike in circles in front of his stoop
working out the terrible thing

    The idler who died in his room all morning, goes out
for a walk
Everyone is glad to be moving
                      like dogs who chase after a stick
The soccer players come kicking straight from work
The sun is weaker over Central Park
Runners, dogwalkers, already the silver body

        is seen above the ballfield
        on a pallid blue sky . The sodium lamps
        light up one by one
          along the path by the lake.   Drivers
          notice the lamps challenging the sun,
          and reach for their headlights, to be
          on the safe side

Stubborn hour that won't make up its mind

                    You will follow the sun
as if it were kissing you personally, you will feel kissed
and happy and depressed until the last niggardly change of
daylight falls across your hands   like a farmer in the
middle ages   then you'll go and sit inside in the dark
grow accustomed to it

Men come home from work with the New York Post in their arms

playing father to a newspaper
                        Women run for buses
as if expecting sudden rain   to wash away their dinner dates

    Indian Summer, a good time to make plans.
When the sun goes down everybody feels alone

In the Dentist's Chair

Here I sit in my dentist's chair,
My eyelids shut against the light;
They say that any moment can yield delight
If you will only look at it bare.

I wish I had the knack.
My mind is tired and young.
I can barely turn over my tongue
As she scrapes away the plaque.

It is November, 4:35, and already night.
A smear of sunset crosses the trees like a far-off scream.
The workmen are warming their hands on the steam
and drinking coffee, under a green traffic light.

I could be one of those workmen. . . .
Well, so what?
You could be a baron, an old porter, but you're not.
Don't let's drool sentimentally over them.

Through a plate glass window I see Central Park;
My head is groggy with fatigue;
Muzak segués from "Hey Jude" to Edvard Grieg.
The Christmas shoppers rush home in the dark.

"Open your mouth?" Doctor Anna's voice interrupts
Distantly, like an upstairs opera singer practising scales.
I widen my mouth. She leans her female
Body over mine, brushing up.

I imagine throwing my arms around her
And pulling her down to my chest.
Nothing so drastic as sex undressed;
I'm too supine to be anything but a nuzzler.

Why muddy this delicacy with pornography?
I'm content to smell her cocoanut soap,
The blue nose-mask so close I can reach up
And touch it with a baby's hand and see

Me reflected in her brown eyes,
Helpless and tiny.
Her Indonesian concentration, skin so shiny. . .
If only she would look at me once with surprise!

She must think me the least of her patients.
I forget to keep my mouth open wide
And irregularly neglect the four roads to gum pride—
The floss, the brush, the red dye and the Stimudents.

"Now let me see how you brush," she directs me,
And hands me a brush as though I were a child.
I wriggle the bristles fast and wild,
Eager to fail and have her correct me.

"You must make circular motions — Here,"
Anna brushes me; "and don't forget *backs* of the teeth.
Run your tongue underneath.
You feel how rough it is there?"

"Your tongue is your most reliable guide."
I poke around those neglected interiors
That taste as though I had eaten cinders
From Krakatoa, and dust from a landslide.

This tongue I carry everywhere with me,
I could be using constantly to ferret little nooks
Where the brush has overlooked!
Only I know I won't. I'm lazy.

Besides, I feel I've made enough concessions.
Let my teeth fall into rags!
I won't become their slaves. And if she nags
Me any more, I'll tell them what I think of their profession.

Fanatical mechanics with their self-righteous airs —
Anti-Communists of the mouth, waging Holy War on plaque,
I wouldn't be surprised if it were all a quack!
And a century from now, some bright Lavoisier

Will come along and prove
That plaque was an illusion, like phlogiston.
— Calm down, you're begging the question.
It's your reflex perversity you so love —

That habit of cranky refusal;
I've lived with it so long,
Like a favorite opinion one later learned was wrong
But can't help lapsing into its espousal.

How strange how each of us resists the good,
In this or that, for spite. Some deny
Their flesh or stay in jobs that suck them dry,
While I cling to bad teeth and bachelorhood.

Okay, shut up. Pay attention to the office.
There's the glaring lamp, and on the wall
Laminated certificates from dental school:
Academy of Implants, Department of Naval Service,

A Seminar in Dallas — most are Doctor Klein's.
A few are Anna's. Backed with plastic or maybe plywood. . ?
They'd laminate their toe-dirt if they could.
Then there's that "painting" — an abstract design

Of mountains, like teeth, to cover a raw edge.
Stay focused outside. Outside, a bird's wing
Flittering; flying to keep from shivering.
The magazines I'll never get to on the window ledge;

The bird in the tree the needle in the gums,
A dry tickling, need to swallow,
The gurgling faucet at my elbow,
My jaws held open with her thumbs. . . .

She nicked me and apologized.
The cut's not painful enough
To blot out everything but itself.
Present can't fill me; still room to fantasize,

Mind rolling back somewhere. Where is it?
Oh yes. The anatomy lesson. How easily
A knife cuts through men's flesh. We
Were being taken through the dissecting room on a visit.

Glenn was anxious to show off his cadaver.
The man's skin had turned olive-green
And rubbery like boiled chicken, and his penis leaned
Handsomely large to one side, awaiting the cleaver.

"Look at this!" another medical student yelled
From two tables down. They pressed around him.
He had struck upon a surgical pin
In his corpse's kneecap, which held

The joints in place. "Keep cutting!"
Someone said, "Let's see the rest."
The scalpel slid as into an overdone roast.
The unresisting muscles parted, exhibiting

A shiver of aluminum. They were spellbound,
As if they'd come upon a will that named them heirs.
"Whoever did it knew his stuff," I heard one swear.
"It must have been a war-time wound!"

I keep returning to that morbid scene —
What's wrong with me tonight? *What's bugging you?*
What are you feeling? A little blue,
I guess. A little down. Melancholy, serene

Like the world in its final hour,
When Matter gives off a modest blush,
The last vital, grey flush on the backs of fish
Flopping in ice. And the gloomy water-tower;

The boulevards in their Viennese decline;
The melon-colored streets at daybreak, looking over-ripe;
Gusts from the river; the broken water-pipes
Flooding the sidewalks with immaculate design.

All of it studied, decomposed, composed, mad:
A manginess more ordered than great art;
I love this state of mind that lets me see each thing apart.
My one last wish is to remain even and sad.

If only I could stay this way forever
Looking calmly out at the plate glass,
I could put up with the coldness and the loss
And be happy knowing I'd be happy — never.

But is that true? Why do I keep
Saying I want to be sad, merely because I
Am? You'll end up making a virtue of every sigh,
And think each letdown is helping you grow deep!

This aesthetics of sadness is a pain in the ass!
There must be something better than this tepid remake,
The cold enjoyment men of introspection take
In re-imagining the world brick by brick as it is.

I want more! One major passion,
And all my meditations can jump out the window.
Make me happy, God; I'll take the risk of being shallow.
I want to kiss the damp earth like a Russian!

Admit it: I'm disappointed. Horrible.
I had expected more. It's all too bland.
(So why is this so hard to understand?
You wanted more, and now you're miserable.)

The girl who charmed me with her feverish effervescence
Is getting married to a walking librium pill.
She who loved large gestures, loved me until
She gave way to an itch for evanescence.

The sorcery of disappearing love
Always distresses and arouses me.
But in fact it is no mystery.
Any judge of character can tell when someone is about to leave.

Then disappointment is all one's fault? You mean,
if I had judged the beloved right on target,
Without fantasies, there'd be no reason to be upset,
Feel rejected or angry at the parting scene?

I've judged intimates correctly and still felt done in.
Foreknowledge and disappointment run on separate tracks.
What's so good about predicting the crumbling from the
                                        cracks?
In the end would I feel any less chagrined?

It's not as if I've been betrayed at every turn.
People have loved me, licked me with their warm fidelity.
In some funny way none of it touches me.
I'm still here playing solitaire on the mind's green lawn.

"Ah, tomorrow you'll feel better. You're just spent.
You've run around all week, giving orders, alert,
And you come here to a chair where you're forced to be inert:
Of course you're set upon by every stray lament!

All the urges you'd suppressed to get your work done,
They're jumping up and throwing their weight around.
A good night's sleep, and you'll feel much more sound."
Despair and Optimism — see how they run.

I get tired chasing them. Neither is me.
Giving myself pep talks, perking up the troops,
And allowing myself an occasional day-off to mope.
Is there any *me* beyond this rapid change of strategy?

"Rinse out please." I spit
Surprising embryos of blood into a suction cup;
I can't keep saliva from dribbling up
My face, I'm turning into a drooling idiot.

I bend and rinse again for good measure.
My stomach almost gags on the taste
Of that green, gritty, peppermint polishing paste.
She watches with what I imagine to be displeasure.

"Today was only a scraping and a cleaning
To remove the pileup. You had plenty of tartar,"
She starts to scold me. The door is ajar
And, tanned from a conference in Texas, Klein comes in
                                              gleaming.

"How's my boy doing?" Anna falls silent.
He is the Jove of the office, she only his assistant.
She does the routine work, he the tricky implants.
"You look as if you've been in an accident,"

Klein laughs. This is his idea of professional wit.
"How are you coming along?"
I try to speak but my mouth is still all tongue.
"It looks all right," says Anna, seeing fit

To shelter me from the father's wrath —
Or is it to protect herself? In any case,
She has given me a moment's grace
Before he can unearth the guilty truth.

"Let's see his X-rays. I'm just curious. . . .
Hm. Not bad for cavities. How about the gums?"
He lifts my lip up with his thumbs.
"You call this — 'all right'?" Klein is furious.

"Those gums look awfully beefy!
We're gonna have to do better than that!
You're flirting with peridonitis, friend — gum rot.
You'll have to play ball with us, or face surgery.

"We can't do it all for you, hold your hand,
We can't go to your house every morning."
His face is breaking out in hives of warning.
Next he remembers to bully the good Anna.

73

"These X-rays are too cloudy. Oh, they're legible
But not razor-sharp. Lacking in contour."
And he explains his point with a metaphor
From childhood games: "Why go for a single

When you can hit the ball out of the park?"
(Which means nothing to this Indonesian woman).
Still, I understand his need to rub it in:
A perfectionist making others toe the mark.

In this, Klein is gross caricature of me:
The lifelong insecurity of Ivy League men
Who have passed all exams, and then
Keep wheedling a higher grade from sluggish Humanity.

She's close to tears — or am I imagining that?
Like a child who's scolded and feels
A sore throat coming on, she conceals
Her swallows while he explains the art.

Her eyes are dark and now she moves her glance
To the cool white counter and the swabs,
To the cupful of scissors, as one day she might stab
Her all-knowing boss in the forehead in a trance.

Klein fails to understand he has gone too far.
I am watching them both, when suddenly,
She reaches for a toothbrush and gives it to me.
A second later, as if by signal, he is out the door.

A new toothbrush, a gift of the management
Which delights me, though the cynic thinks from habit:
"At these prices they can afford it."
I put on my overcoat, and wave goodbye to the arrangements.

The Last Slow Days of Summer

"BE YOUR OWN MASTER!" says the Vedanta Society sign.
Why not?. . . In the park
Some clouds roll over me like Greenland on a map.
If I wanted to I could imagine I was flying over
The Greenland coast and gazing down at the white fjords.
Instead I'm lying on the grass, listening to city sounds.
They come to me in three-dimensional form,
Like a loaf of Wonder Bread. Baby carriages squeak
Near the middle. Cars humming through Central Park,
Somewhere near the back of the loaf.
What sound would be the end-piece, the round brown sliver?
The unzipping of airline bags.
Or a glove thwacked
By a rookie pitcher who falls apart
In the eighth inning. The manager takes the ball silently,
Like a man who has eaten a full loaf of bread
And has a stomach pain. Don't glamorize silence.
There is nothing profound about quiet, it is usually
Only the universe holding its stomach.

Delmore Schwartz must have been a great talker.
They say he put most of his talent into his life
But I don't know, I think his prose is pretty great;
He made a better storywriter than a poet.
I could write a thousand-page biography
Propounding that stance, and interview all the old rummy
    critics
At the New York Times like Anatole Broyard, powerful now;
They would let their hair down about Delmore,
And the final crackup.
The reason I'm thinking of Delmore Schwartz is that
he wrote a poem about city parks. And it wasn't that
    successful,
It went on for about twelve pages, but I admired him
For writing a poem with so little point,

And so much prosy description. I think he was trying to
Eulogize normal middle-class happiness on a Sunday
     afternoon,
And how he felt out of it. But that wouldn't have
Taken twelve pages. . . . He was probably being ironic
About the people's happiness, and secretly thought
They weren't happy. He wrote it about the same time
Robert Moses was carving out his parks empire
By forcing the Long Island millionaires to give up their privacy
So that the middle class could get to the beach.
Of course it was also supposed to benefit
The poor slum-dwellers, but how many of them
Ever made it to Sunken Meadows?
Or Jones Beach?

What's strange about parks — innocent greenery —
Is that no one ever suspected them to ruin New York.
Yet what finally gutted the city were the parkways
Moses built, slashed through all five boroughs
Quiet lower-middle-class neighborhoods bulldozed
For cars to get to the picnic grounds faster,
Or the Hamptons —
A life of paperwork capped by a summer home.
But I can't blame them: I'd like a summer home myself!
I don't really believe New York is dying, no more than
The universe is dying. I have no stake in seeing
This poem end pessimistically.
I'd like to leave people with a good feeling.

Robert Moses, Delmore Schwartz.
Two ambitious Jews, like myself.
They tried to be their own masters. . . .
It's hard to imagine New York going under
On a slow summer day like today
Without even a loud noise to mark it
Like the Empire State Building keeling over
And everyone running to the scene of default.
The helicopters will be standing by,

Ready to take us to Greenland.
A special airlift for artistic and poetic men of letters,
A jumbo Boeing crammed to the teeth,
And you can't get in if your name isn't
Listed in Poets and Writers Directory.
"So long, New York School of Poets!"
I'll stay behind, tending the weeds
And sleeping in deserted Central Park.
Soon I'll be hearing about the Godthaab School:
Their seemingly infinite talent for "chatty brilliance,"
Buddhism, and marathon readings.
I'll shake my head and sigh: What are
Anne and Michael doing now?
How was this year's big Hallowe'en party,
Or do they even celebrate Hallowe'en in Greenland?
Maybe they're into solstice holidays, like Midsummer Night.

The Truth That Hurts

Funny how when I think back now
To how I was at college, I can't
Distinguish me from all the rest;
We're sitting down at Rikers,
With one white counter snaking
Through the stools,
Eavesdropping on the loud girl telling
About her suicide attempt with razors
To her embarrassed friend.
It sounded all too familiar.
Suicide was like a garden of spices
For the blind, that we visited
From time to time with our eyes
Open, sampling the air.

Our lives, like the black-and-white
Films we could never resist,
Were grainy, harsh as sixteen millimeter
Blown up to thirty-five.
We liked it that way: austere.
But no — we wanted more, we never
Tired of saying it; and the more was
Each other that we could tell this to.
We told each other all.
Those were the days we had such an itch
To confide, and what hurt most seemed truest.
Only a confidence could arouse
The acrid precise, like the smell
Of a lit match held between two sets of eyes.
Time stops when you say what
You thought you never could,
And here you are still breathing like a courtier at the Borgias.

Now I begin to pick me out a bit:
I was the one who came from Brooklyn slums,

And never wanted my roommates to forget it.
But they took me in without making a fuss
About social class, which chagrined me.
I fell in with the literary set,
And by junior year I'd gotten my desk
At the college magazine, *Columbia Review*,
With my own swivel-chair that I loved
moving round in without standing up.
That was the game: to answer the phone like
A paraplegic wheeling over to behind the desk:
"Hello? Review!"

In my senior year I was Editor-in-chief.
In the bottom drawers of my desk I'd find
Chocolate pudding dishes from the lunchroom,
That I traced to a bearded sophomore poet
Who had horrible broken front teeth
And a demented way of not looking at you
While singing throaty, countertenor madrigals.
He also wrote epic poems about
Jewish cemeteries. One day I caught him:
Burst in as he was applying
A spoonful of pudding to his beard.
Bashful smile (relieved at being caught?)
The others were crazier.
And so I flourished.

II

Jon and I were sitting on the grass
Behind the Metropolitan Museum;
He asked me didn't I mind the loss
Of Nature, and the separation
Between cities and lakes trees brooks?
Didn't I mind the concrete everywhere?
I said I loved it; Loss was for the academics.
He took my narrowness for courage.

That was my way: I backed up prejudices strong.
People with more culture than I
Were shaken. Years later, they quoted
These statements back to me as turning-points
In their lives, and I was apalled.
Did I say that bunk? What provincialism.
Nevertheless I was pleased.

Always pleased to make an impression on people.
Arrogance trumps uncertainty; I talked my way
Into jobs I knew nothing about, because
Some knew even less.
When push comes to shove, an insight
Can be teased from a particular;
And wisdom, approached as a tonal problem,
Reduced to a set of dots and reproduced.

III

I give my opinions out for a fee now.
A roving consultant, I go on nerve,
Till one day, at a rural university
Whose new glass study center is sunk in snow
I see myself ponderously crossing a windy campus
After a faculty luncheon that's bloated me
And Professor DuB—is taking me by the arm;
Yes I'll talk my head off, must give them a good show,
While all I'm thinking is
The turkey strand between my teeth, if I could only work it
    out;
And my feet getting frozen in the snow.
My audience stirs as I walk through the door.
I see the podium of rich blonde wood,
Oh, and the automatic blackboard-screen
That disappears at the push of a button!

The walls are *art brut* modern, fired brick,
And the floors made with grey slats of concrete

That a prisoner could tear his hands on for centuries.
I stare from the pit at the tilted red aisles, a steep lookup
To the top row. No clock in back.
I pace. I talk. I cry. I'm brilliant
And the crowd laughs. I make it into a song
As I go along, I make up my little song:
A little audacity, a little skepticism
And real-life anecdotes that warm the house.
Always pleased to have an effect on people.
Only now they want to know
Where I got my facts.

"You still haven't answered my question,"
Taunts the lanky young man in the brown corduroy jacket
In the next to the last row, and whatever I say
Makes him slump even further in his seat.
"I don't care for your constant use of the masculine gender,"
A woman in front objects.—"Give us more details!"—
"How can we trust you when you're not specific enough?"

If I keep still their anger will go away.
For starters I'll agree: yes, well
The problem *is* complex
And we must break for lunch.
But the room stays very tense.
And there's nothing I can do to remove it,
Their resentment comes from a deeper source,
They want answers for their lives,
There is nothing I can do.

IV

"You want people to adore you,"
Said my last girlfriend, analyzing our breakup.
"You try to get people to adore you
And people oblige (they do when you make that
Need clear enough, that's why you're successful);
But you keep them at a distance when it comes to love

Because you can't give back equal love.
Oh—you're incredibly supportive;
But that supportiveness is the expression
Of your guilt for not being able to love them.
I'm not saying you couldn't love anyone,
But it's you who thinks that you can't,
Doubts that you can, so you help people instead.
By being everyone's support, it's also a way
To stay in command.

"Actually there's nothing wrong with wanting Adoration
And Power. They're great," she said.
"It's your guilty conscience that spoils it.
Why are you so guilty? Your guilt's what muddies everything."

I agreed; it was probably true.
"And that's another thing," she went on;
"You're willing to admit criticism of yourself,
But you do it just to take the credit for openness,
And it stays on a purely verbal level.
You don't really take it into yourself.
You only like the pose of confessing
Wrongdoing; you like it so much that it
Completely bypasses your heart.
You think you're perfect; that's your problem."

That's not so, I said.
Sometimes I take criticism to heart
And I've let myself be changed by it.
There are times when I'm not defensive.
There are also certainly other times when I am.

"That's my final point!" she cried.
"My final point is that you qualify everything!
Your favorite way of countering criticism
Is to say: 'Well to some extent yes, not always.'
That's how you deaden the truth that hurts."

October 7, 1975

82

The Daily Round

To Mandelstam

Last cup of coffee,
Go slowly through the day
Pick up the laundry on the way home from work
Walk slowly through the grimy streets
This is your last chance to see this life

See how the sunlight beats against the curtains
Trying to force its way in
Defeated by a thin green rag,
Its knuckles weaken and it falls to the cement
I can watch them for hours
Leaning on my pillow
Without lifting a finger to help

My God, how I love this world

Remember that the sun is yellow
No matter what they try to tell you
Remember times of peace
When the Brillo Pad drools
Against a warm dish
Remember that you said, "But I love
This poor earth, because I have not seen another"
Remember how the sky is grey or pink or black
And that her hair falls straight across her back
When you hear the passkey turning in the lock.

OTHER BOOKS AVAILABLE FROM *SUN*

Love Wounds & Multiple Fractures: Poems, by Carolanne Ely
    ISBN 0-915342-02-2 (paperback).

The Eyes Don't Always Want to Stay Open: Poems, by
Phillip Lopate
    ISBN 0-915342-12-X (paperback).
    ISBN 0-915342-13-8 (hardcover).

Blue Springs: Poems, by Michael O'Brien
    ISBN 0-915342-06-5 (paperback).
    ISBN 0-915342-09-X (hardcover).

Toujours l'amour: Poems, by Ron Padgett
    ISBN 0-915342-10-3 (paperback).
    ISBN 0-915342-11-1 (hardcover).

How I Wrote Certain of My Books, by Raymond Roussel
Translated from the French, with notes and a bibliography, by
Trevor Winkfield.
    ISBN 0-915342-95-7 (paperback).

Lauds: Poems, by Harvey Shapiro
    ISBN 0-915342-01-4 (paperback).
    ISBN 0-915342-07-3 (hardcover).

Theories of Rain and Other Poems, by Bill Zavatsky
    ISBN 0-915342-03-0 (paperback).
    ISBN 0-915342-08-1 (hardcover).

Address inquiries and catalogue requests to
SUN, 456 Riverside Drive, New York, N.Y. 10027